Hi Friend

Diane Reyes

BookLeaf Publishing

Presentation by *BookLeaf Publishing*

Web: www.bookleafpub.com

E-mail: info@bookleafpub.com

ISBN: 9789357216234

First edition 2023

DEDICATION

To Ink

Mirrors

Sea and Sky mirror;
Reveal Truth of the other.
My Soul in your eyes

Good

If you rise early
And work very hard
Deny the ache for
Silly, playful joy
Still tides of feeling
Reshape molten soul
Exchange contentment
For compulsive drive
Cover, color your
Ever changing face
Commit. Chizzle your
Tormented corpse for
Inspiration a
Marble monument
Hope against unknown
Constant and useful
Eternally safe.
At last you are Good.
Nothing like you were.
And nothing like me.

Ink

The ink in my veins
From heart to hand, changes, fills
This stolen blue Bic.

This Too

I shrike at the sky
The trees breathe slow and whisper
Love, this too shall pass.

Be Still

don't fear solitude,
silence - the everyday deaths.
what's true awakens.

Rumination

Rabid rage to no avail;
No satisfaction's found.
The enemy before me stands;
Unmoved, untouched, unbowed.

Then in a blink the dream dissolves.
The monster was within.
Crackling flames inside my mind-
Ashamed- quiet and dim.

Deep breaths and ancient wisdom soothe,
"This moment's all there is"
And should I start to slip and dream,
Freedom's gained with a list:

5 things my eyes can see around
4 things my hands can feel
3 sounds (the fan, a bird, my voice)
2 smells, 1 taste: all real.

My art, desk, books, my toys, and notes,
Non-judging, seem to say:
"We waited for you, welcome home.
All's well, my friend, you're safe."

Surprise

The field was empty
But for loose rocks and barbed wire.
Then, a green Winter.

Ambition

Forget Ambition
Its lonely, treacherous path.
Just be curious.

Enough

Bewildered she says,
"I guess you don't want to money"
The truth: I don't want.

Authenticity

The Sun, brilliant, bright,
Never asks if you're worthy
Or if it is Good.

Luck

"Pick up every coin"
Each one reminds me of you.
Heads, Tails...I'm lucky.

Fly

Fly! Witness the Sky-
Abundant and beautiful.
A miniature Soul.

IDK

"I don't know" is said
Sadly like surrender. But
It's the beginning.

Comfort

I, broken hearted,
took the trees' advice: "Sit still."
The world came and went.

Weasel

I wish I'd told you:
I don't care who loves you.
I care that you're loved.

Acceptance

Accept this will end.
Witness with courage, patience.
You are changing too.

Home

Old trees are ground up;
Become seedling nurseries.
Home, heaven...right here.

Resistance

Nature always says:
"What's free transforms, and lives on."
We resist and die.

Dandelion

A dandelion
sprouts in a field of asphalt.
Grow where you're planted.

Prost

We're sitting beside a castle
some hot, lazy afternoon
In Germany.
Just us, a tree,
and two glasses of cheap white wine.
Our language is bankrupt
except for two pence phrases.
Yet, enough.
A bell tolls.
You say, "maybe...wedding."
We look each other in the eye.
Our glasses kiss.
Clouds yawn and stretch.
The tree whispers to itself.

On the occasion
I am so humbled to pray,
I close my eyes,
labor up the hill,
to the bistro table.
Between our words
Beyond our worlds,
By the castle in the mountains,
Beneath the Sun...
And I sit beside my friend.

Love

Love is: Guinea pigs,
hugs, candy, books, dinosaurs,
"Have you drank water?"

www.ingramcontent.com/pod-product-compliance
Lightning Source LLC
Chambersburg PA
CBHW051721130826
49812CB00034B/1291
* 9 7 8 9 3 5 7 2 1 6 2 3 4 *